The Poetry of Laurence Binyon

Volume IX - Auguries

Robert Laurence Binyon, CH, was born on August 10th, 1869 in Lancaster in Lancashire, England to Quaker parents, Frederick Binyon and Mary Dockray.

He studied at St Paul's School, London before enrolling at Trinity College, Oxford, to read classics.

Binyon's first published work was Persephone in 1890. As a poet, his output was not prodigious and, in the main, the volumes he did publish were slim. But his reputation was of the highest order. When the Poet Laureate, Alfred Austin, died in 1913, Binyon was considered alongside Thomas Hardy and Rudyard Kipling for the post which was given to Robert Bridges.

Binyon played a pivotal role in helping to establish the modernist School of poetry and introduced imagist poets such as Ezra Pound, Richard Aldington and H.D. (Hilda Doolittle) to East Asian visual art and literature. Most of his career was spent at The British Museum where he produced many books particularly centering on the art of the Far East.

Moved and shaken by the onset of the World War I and its military tactics of young men slaughtered to hold or gain a few yards of shell-shocked mud Binyon wrote his seminal poem *For the Fallen*. It became an instant classic, turning moments of great loss into a National and human tribute.

After the war, he returned to the British Museum and wrote numerous books on art; especially on William Blake, Persian and Japanese art.

In 1931, his two volume Collected Poems appeared and in 1933, he retired from the British Museum.

Between 1933 and 1943, Binyon published his acclaimed translation of Dante's *Divine Comedy* in an English version of terza rima.

During the Second World War Binyon wrote another poetic masterpiece *'The Burning of the Leaves'*, about the London Blitz.

Robert Laurence Binyon died in Dunedin Nursing Home, Bath Road, Reading, on March 10th, 1943 after undergoing an operation.

Index of Contents

A PRELUDE AT EVENING

My spirit was like the lonely air
Before night.
Like hovering cloud that's melted there
In the late light,
When slow the vast earth-shadows reach
To the last flush,
And the wandering Silences have each
Their own hush.

Did the green grass about me glimmer,
Or trees tower?
Not softer to my sense, nor dimmer.
The obscure power
Of all the world's wide trouble, fought
In the heart's recess:
My heart was solitude, my thought
Emptiness.

But through my spirit that seemed, unfilled,
Alone to float,
A sudden dewy sweetness thrilled;
A low note!
And then a loud note, rippling full
To a still pause:

The liquid silence was a pool
That a breeze flaws.

It throbbed again, how lonely clear!
A song that seemed
Sprung beyond memory or fear,
A voice dreamed
In a land that no man ever found;
And who knows
What shook those lingering drops of sound
At the rich close?

Ah, where were you, passion and grief
Of the world's wrong?
What had you to do with a trembling leaf
And a bird's song.
And spaces calm with coming of night,
And the fresh gloom
Of shadowy trees, and smelt delight
Of hidden bloom?

Yet O, in me that song had part
Because of you!
It drank of the very blood of the heart
It quivered through
Because of the tears of joy, and the cost
Of a joy's breath,
Measureless thoughts of a dearness lost,
Hope, and death.

Strangeness of longing, beauty, pain!
I was aware
Of all your secret, soft as rain.
In the dim air.
For Life it was that sang aloud
To the lone dew.
Brave in the night and sweet in the cloud;
My heart knew.

MALHAM COVE

I

There is threat in the wind, and a murmur of water that swells
Swift in the hollow: about me a shadow is thrown;
For above is no valley sequestered in shy, green dells,

But abrupt, sky-closing, a wall and a vastness of stone.
Did the rock split asunder with ages? or suddenly smote
The hand of a God on the mountain? for under the face
Of the imminent height, at the humid and cold rock-base,
From out of the dungeoned recesses, the cavernous throat,
Disimprisoned there bursts, not a rill, not a trickle of spray,
But broad in its gushing and full and sweeping apace
A river arisen that dances in laughter away.

II

Builded aloof; unscaleable; towering stark
To the fugitive cloud and the blue, O Soul of the Rock!
Silent, remote as the moon, that will'st not to hark
To the cry of the lamb on the precipice lost from the flock;
If thou suffer the pine in thy cranny that dizzily clings
Small-seen as a fern, or a thicket of obstinate thorn,
'Tis disdain that neglects them, rather a scorning of scorn,
Unheedful of them as of those irresistible springs
Gushing out from beneath thee, unheard as the cry of the bird
That skims from the shadow and hovers a flashing of wings
Mid the flush and the greening of April.—
Thou standest unstirred,

III

A desert uplifted, a desert where bones rot and bleach,
A barrenness knowing not change nor date nor event,
A strength without speech, without motion, yet stronger than speech;
A bulk without feature, a winter of force long spent;
And neither is hope, nor terror, nor weakness there.
But a pressure and weight of oblivion where no man is known,
Nor feature from feature distinguished but all overthrown;
Like the rampart of Time that confronts us enormous and bare,
Immuring the dream and the vision whereby we have breath;
Like Night and the end of the light to them that despair:
I stand in thy shadow and fear thee, thou stature of Death!

IV

Come away, come away! There is light in the water that glides.
Come away with the water that hastes from the heart of the hills,
A sinuous ripple that sings and that nowhere abides.
But broken, a murmuring sparkle, on ledges and sills
Of the rock, as it swerves, carries in it a wavering fire.

Like a thought, like a joy, that no barrier stays from its flight.
Or a dance of young children that carol their heart of delight;
For it calls to the bud to burst open, the blade to thrust higher;
To my heart, to ray heart, it is calling — "O follow! for here
Is thine own heart, quick and enamoured of love and of light;
O follow my swiftness and stay not in shadows of fear!"

V

On beds in the valley, on sunny half-islanded banks,
Where roots are athirst and refreshed and saplings grow bold
Bowing their youth to the breezes in quivering ranks.
Primroses, a cluster of softness and fragrance, unfold;
And the fairy anemone, shaking her blossoms agleam —
They are kisses of light as they tremble to touch and to part —
Is flushed, ah! how faint, as with fire from the innermost heart
Of a world in whose veins is a laughter as clear as the stream;
And the music upholds me, enchants me, and borne like a wave,
I am melted, I flow, I am nought but a hope and a dream,
And in me is the youth of the flowers, and grief in her grave.

VI

Sudden a gust flings a shadow! and shivering, the black
Driven leaves at the roots of the oak-tree are whirled up and lost
Like the wild thoughts of fear into darkness, and strong boughs crack.
And a gloom rushes down with a wailing, and out of it tossed
Pale snow is outshaken, and hail drops icily keen
On young leaf and dead; and awakened in tree-tops aloud
Is the roar of the storm that has gathered the hills in a shroud
Until naught of the towering rock but in glimmers is seen.
A vision unfeatured, a phantom of terrible birth: —
Is it thou that appearest, a presence divined in the cloud,
Thy ribs and thy knees and thy breasts, O Titaness Earth?

VII

Is it thine, the great voice that confuses the winds and the floods
In a meaningless cry as of madmen, a blindness of wrath,
Smiting the bosses of oak and the virginal buds.
Negligent where thou hast beaten thy desolate swath?
O thou, who hast armed as for battle thy creatures wild
With fierceness of claw and of fang, of hoof and of horn.
From thee, even thee, from thy heart-beat was man, too, born
With flesh like a flower defenceless? is he thy child?

In whose eyes are wonder and trouble, who strikes, yet the wrong
He has done he turns from again and with sorrow is torn:
How shall his heart be as thine or in thy way strong?

VIII

For who that is born of a woman has known not the hour
When the spirit within him is daunted and this world comes
As an army against him, a terror of alien power.
And fate, too vast to be borne, his courage benumbs?
Lost he seems as a child upon mountains alone.
Who has longed not then with longing for a strength past pain
To endure the rending of sorrow that makes hope vain.
To be kneaded in iron and stubborned in armour of stone?
That hour when the heavens are shaken within the mind,
And the world is an enemy armed have I not known?
For the strength of the stony mountain have I not pined?

IX

But lo! on a sudden, with sighing the storm ends now
In a radiant relenting: golden the light reappears
With a glory of drops that are dancing on leaf and on bough;
And a music, a wandering music returns to my ears.
From the primrose is breathing a freshness, and wild, shy smells
From the moss, where the snowflake is melted to dazzling dew.
And the voice of the birds on the banks is uplifted anew
To the carolling voice of the river that onward swells.
Onward away, where the buds gleam white on the tree!
The rain and the gloom are forgotten in heaven's young blue;
And my heart flows otit with the river, the river with me.

X

In a trance, in a trance I listen; and into my soul,
As it draws far back to a stillness darkly stored
With infinite sound, gather and gradual roll
The voices of all the torrents on earth outpoured.
"We tarry not, rest not, sleep not," aloud they cry,
"We are swift as the hours that crumble thy strength into dust;
We build thee no home, nor a fortress wherein to trust;
But in us is the sound of dominion falling from high,
And the kings of the world dethroned and towers laid bare.
We move, we are ever beyond; we change, we die;

We laugh, we live; to follow wilt thou too dare? "

How shall I not go with you, waters swift?
Too long in yesterday's self I tarry, and keep
The dust of the world about me. Uplift, uplift.
Lose me, a wave in the waves that laugh and leap!
Lo, into uttermost time my thoughts I send:
And because in my heart is a flowing no hour can bind.
Because through the wrongs of the world looking forth and behind,
I find for my thought not a close, for my soul not an end.
With you will I follow, nor crave the strength of the strong
Nor a fortress of time to enshield me from storms that rend.
This is life, this is home, to be poured as a stream, as a song.

ELEGY

The little waves fall in the wintry light
On idle sands, along the bitter shore.
The piling clouds are all a pale suspended flight;
They tarry and are moved no more.

Thin rushes tremble about the naked dune;
A hovering sail sinks down the utmost sea;
With wreckage and old foam the unending sands are strewn;
And the waves heap their dumbness over me.

This is the Earth that lasts beyond our dreams
Of time, and rushing onward without rest,
Deludes us with her trancing silences, yet teems
Fiercely, and burns within her breast,

Insatiate of youth, this old, old Earth,
Who uses our spent ashes for her need,
Shaping the delicate marvel of her youngest birth,
And still she kindles a new seed.

Intent on the unborn creature of her thought
And busy in the waste: O even here,
Though masked as in a calm of dumb frustration, naught
Stays her, no pang nor any fear,

But subtly, with a touch invisible,
She is changing and compelling; and me too.

Me too, upon the secret stream of that deep will
She moves to a destiny ever new.

And yet this hour my spirit hides its face.
And, backward turned, sighs out an idle pain
For the remembered paths these feet may not retrace
And the hours that cannot come again.

O hours of heavenly madness in delight
That felt the swiftness and the throb of wings,
That stole the burning soul of naked summer night
And the moons of the perfumed springs!

Not now to you my longing stretches hands,
But to lost hours, that had no fruit, no seed.
Like fading of low light beyond forgotten lands,
They have passed and are dead indeed.

And once, for once, unrecking Earth, you seem
With me to linger and to acquiesce.
To share the desolation of my doubt and dream,
And to ponder upon barrenness.

The wind lulls on the waste, and has no will.
The foiled tides hush and falter at their bound.
A little sand is blown, then all again is still;
And the clouds hang silence around.

With such an absence felt in the lone skies,
Suppression of such tears, profoundly sprung
In long-remembering looks of unconversing eyes
As when the old bury the young.

THE MIRROR

I

Where is all the beauty that hath been?
Where the bloom?
Dust on boundless wind? Grass dropt into fire?
Shall Earth boast at last of all her teeming womb,
All that suffered, all that triumphed, to inspire
Life in perfect mould and speech, the proud mind's lamp serene —
Nothing? Space be starry in tremendous choir —
For whom?

In this deserted chamber, as the evening falls,
Silent curtains move no fold;
Long has ebbed the floor's pale gold;
Shadows deepen down the silent walls.
The air is mute as dreams beneath a sleeper's face.
Distant, undivined;
But every hovering shadow seems to hold
Want untold.
The look of things forsaken, each in its own place,
Memories without home in any mind.
Idle, rich neglect and perfume old —
Over these the glimmer of the twilight fades;
Infinite human solitude invades
Forms relinquished, hues resigned.

O little mirror, round and clear.
In solemn-coloured shadow lying
Cold as the moon, pale as a tear.
With spiritual silver beam replying
Indifferently to all things as to one;
Beauty's relic and oblivion.
But void, void, void! Desolate as a cave
Abandoned even of the breaking wave,
A home of youth and mirth, when all its guests are gone!
As I touch thee in the silence here,
Where thou liest alone, apart.
Through the silence of my heart
Thou flashest elfin flames of fear.
Like a thought of lost delight,
Like love-sweetness, like despair.
Come faint spices of the night
Floating on the darkened air.
The air is tender with the sense of dew,
Is tranced, is dim, is heavy, as if there hung
Within the tinges of its shadowy hue
Ghosts of lost flowers, with all their petals young.
And the young beauty they made incense to.

O forlorn mirror, is there nothing thine?
The cup is emptied of its fragrant wine,
The dress is vacant of the breathing form,
And thou that gleam'st
All absence of what once moved gracious, white and warm
In thy clear wells, or luminously mused,
O little mirror long disused.
Laid in this empty bower's recess.
Thou thyself seem'st
The soul and mystery of emptiness.

Yet if I should raise thee now,
As once and oft, thou knowest how,
Hand and slim wrist, smooth as a flower-stem, raised
Thy silent brilliance, and with intent brow
Eyes within thee gazed
Seeking thy oracle,
Shall not from those pellucid secrecies appear
Not I, nor any shape of this dim room.
But all that in thy cave of lambent gloom
Hath dwelt and still may dwell.
Ambushed like visions bound in sleeping memory's cell;
All that thy brightness buries as the sea
Tossed bones and crusted gold: had I the key,
Mightst thou not ope thy depths, mightst thou not yield,
Wonder of wonders! What since time began
Was never yet revealed.
The unmapped, unmeasured, secret heart of man?

Half-shut eyes voluptuously
Lightening, as the bosom swells and glows;
Smile to smile flowering from an ardent thought;
what moments didst thou deify
With the promise of life crushed to wine
Redder than the cheek's triumphant rose!
— But from deeper places hast thou brought
Nothing? Are not other answers thine?

Hast thou not heard, hast thou not seen,
Hast thou not shown, hast thou not found
Shames unwhispered, terrors bound.
Earthquake pangs of aghast surmise.
When with itself the heart has been
Face to face in an hour profound?
Out of thee what ghosts shall rise,
Shapes and gestures, and accusing eyes!
World-flattered faces in midnights of pain;
Faces defaced by tiger-lusts insane;
Faces appalled before a self unguessed;
Ashaming dawns on faces fallen and dispossessed!
O what glimpses hast thou flashed in dread,
With what hauntings wast thou visited.
Apparitions of a soul made bare
Shuddering at the thing it looked on there!
But thou art stainless, though the heart has bled,
Thou art silent as the air
Or the wave that closes smooth above the drowner's head.

No man hath seen his soul
Save for a glimpse in the night
Brief as an ember of coal
Blown for an instant bright.
To see his own soul as it is,
Eternity must enter him
With the torches of Seraphim
That have shone to the last abyss.
Mirror, couldst thou show the spirit this.
Then within this narrow room
Were the Judgment and the Doom.
For by so much as its own self it knew
Searched by that burning vision through and through
To the innermost of where it crouched and hid
Amid the husks of the mean deeds it did.
Amid the shadow of all it shunned, the quest
It turned from, and in palterings acquiesced,
To the uttermost of what its eager passion
Caught of the glory springing to re-fashion
Hope and the world, and great with pity saw
Life darkly wrestling with the angel, Law —
By such a measure, molten in that fire.
Should the soul mete itself on God's desire,
Suffer at last all wisdom, and endure
The beam and vision of a thought all-pure.
O were not this to taste Heaven's dawn, or dwell,
Because of knowledge, in the pains of Hell?

II

Where is all the wailing, all the want
That sorrow tore
From Love's bleeding breast? Extinguished quite?
Shall the wide-winged glory of hope extravagant,
Shall the laughter, shall the song that sprang to soar
Fall, and no ear hearken, and their failing flight
Echoless waste walls of adamant
Ignore?

Draw wide the curtain! Fabulous, remote
Night is come.
Over Earth's lost bosom fragrant breathings float
Into glimmering heights of gloom.
But upon the solitary verge extreme
Steals a beam.
Hushed and sudden, ere the eye could note,
Lo, the moon is there!

Innocence of splendour, gazing bare,
Drenches leaves in quiet, thought in dream.
Is it Earth's pale mirror lifted lone
For an answer to her million sighs?
Can that far Tranquillity atone
In the gaze of those unnumbered eyes
For the pang and for the moan,
For the heart's dim burial and long dirge.
Luring, as she lures the mutinous sea-surge.
To her will of peace this human tide?

From a charmed shadow on the shorn hill-side
Hand-in-hand lovers through the trees emerge.
And pause; their very souls are glorified,
Their feet tread airy on immaterial ground,
With marvelling gaze they feel
That well of spiritual light overflow
The listening hush, and steal
Fear and trouble, as though
The world were one vast music of ethereal sound
And they a stillness in the midst of it.
Peace, peace and pity! pardon, pity, peace,
Passing all mortal wit!
O truth long-sought and magically found,
O wonder and release!
O secret of the world long-hidden in day's dust!
They bathe their hearts in that sweet dew, their hands
Thrill clasping in a touch that understands
Nothing magnificent but a divine surrender
Absolving and august.
To distances immersed and tender
Unfolds this vale of struggle hard and pent,
Region of unwon ravishment
In unadventured lands,
A place of leaves and lonely light and leafy scent
Storied like that old forest of the perilous Fleece.

Sorceress of million nights!
Hast thou charmed indeed the brew,
When with stealth of perverse rites —
Mouths that mutter, hands that strew, —
Love tormented and malign.
Flushed with terror like a maddening wine
Sought another's rue?
Hecate of the cross-roads, hast thou hearkened
To the sailing witch's mew
And the felon raven's croak
When the shuddering winds were darkened

And the leaves rushed from the withered oak?
Ah, not these foul toys would I invoke!
for some supreme enchanting spell,
Voice of a God crying aloud,
Felt and feared on Earth's heart-strings,
To conjm-e and to compel
Like a spectre from the shroud
Or like incense-dust that springs
Into fire and fragrant cloud.
Out of thy blind caves and cold recesses
Out of that blank mirror's desert beam
All the unnumbered longings and wild prayers.
Infinite heart-broken tendernesses.
Indignations and despairs
That from man's long wound of passion stream.
Sucked like vapour, like a mist of tears
Into that imagined peace, that ecstasy!
O surely, surely, thou hast wrought thy part
In every secret and tempestuous heart,
Thou that hast gleamed on thousand battle-crimsoned spears,
Thou that wast radiant on Gethsemane!

She has seen not, she has heard not.
Hearts have leapt for her, but she has stirred not.
Pity she has made, but none has had.
Though her magic mingles with Earth's want
And the trouble of Earth's tender sons,
Thunder of the builded Babylons,
Music of the dreaming poet's chant,
Venture of the steering argosies.
With a light as of divine fulfilment clad
Breathing in for ever syllables of peace.
Peace, is it peace? Yet Earth, dark Earth,
Mother, O Mother, thou that nourishest
In the blind patience of thy teeming breast
Hope without end; who drivest life to birth.
Yet numberest not our dear and sacred dead.
Unheeding of our anguish and lost cries
So thou mayst build beyond us, in our stead,
A race enriched with all for which we bled,
Of haughtier stature and of kinglier eyes;
Thou of whose vast desire strong realms of old,
The dynasty of empires, were but waves
That towered and crashed into their splendid graves.
For thine unresting hunger to remould
Yet mightier, O insatiable! Doth fear
Not shake thee, Mother, seest thou not ev'n here
In that cold mirror's answer what shall steep

Thee also in oblivion? Thou shalt keep
Of all the fruit of thy most fiery spring,
Stored riches of thy sleepless trafficking,
And proud perfection thou hast travailed for,
Nothing! The beauty that thy body bore
Fresh and exulting (Mother, dost not weep?)
Laughter of streams, young flowers, and starry seas.
Pillar and palace, heaven-faced images
That man has wrought, his tossing heart to ease.
Nothing! To cloud shall vanish the deed done;
The bannered victory, the wrong borne alone.
Nothing! and thou be desolate and none
To feel thy desolation: emptiness,
Night within night, immense and issueless,
Till as a breath upon the mirror dies,
Fades the last smoke of thy long sacrifice.

Out of the deeps, trembling, the soul
Cries through night to the silent pole:
"I that am want, I that am grief,
I that am love, I that am mirth,
I that am fear, I that am fire.
Though thou clothe me in beauty brief.
Though I have worn thy sweet attire,
I, thy endless sorrow, Earth,
Dwell in the glory of God's desire,
That kneads for ever in the flesh
Of man, to make his spirit afresh,
A marvel more than all thy wandering seas,
And mightier than thy caverned mysteries,
Nor stays nor sleeps, but world on world transfuses
Melted ever to diviner uses.
Through infinite swift changes burning,
Itself the end, no end discerning,
Till all the universe be wrought
Into its far perfecting thought.
Then this mind of cloud and rue
Shall in eternal mind be new,
Mirror of God, pure and alone,
See and be seen, know and be known."

TO TIME

Time, Time, who choosest
All in the end well;
Who severely refusest

Fames upon trumpets blown
Loud for a day, and alone
Makest truth to excel:

Shadow of God, slowly
Gathering words, long
Scorned, to make them holy.
And deeds like stars bright
That none perceived in the light,
Lifting the weak to be strong:

Shall I not praise thee.
Thou just judge? Yet O
What so long stays thee?
Why must thy feet halt.
While our tears grow salt
And our old hopes go!

Beauty is throned at last;
Truth rings falsehood's knell;
But our strength, our joy is past
While our hearts wait thee
Time, Time, I hate thee.
Hate thee, and rebel.

THE TIGER-LILY

What wouldst thou with me? By what spell
My spirit allure, absorb, compel?
The last long beam that thou didst drink
Is buried now on evening's brink.
The garden's leafy alleys lone,
With shadowy stem and mossy stone,
Intangibly seem now to dress
Colour and odour motionless.
A stealing darkness breathes around.
As if it rose out of the ground.
And tinging into it soft gold
Ebbs, and the dewy green glooms cold,
And dim boughs into black retire.
But thou, seven-throated Flower of Fire,
Sombring all the shadows near thee.
Dost still, as if the night did fear thee,
Glory amid the failing hues
And this invading dusk refuse,
And breathing out thy languid spice

My spirit to thine own entice.

Warm wafts that linger touch my cheek.
What is it in me thou wouldst seek?
Thou meltest all my thoughts away
As leaf on leaf is mingled grey
In shadow on shadow, past discerning.
O cold to touch, to vision burning,
What power is in thee so to change
And my familiar sense estrange?
Thou seemest born within a mind
That has no ken of human kind;
Remote from quick heart, curious brain,
Feeling in joy, thinking in pain.
Remote as beauty of sleeping snow
Is from a flame's wild shredded glow;
Remote from mirth, anger or care.
Or the deep wound and want of prayer.
Yet like some word of splendid speech
Beyond our human hearing's reach,
Whose meaning, could its sound be known,
Might earth's imprisoned secret own
That binds as with a viewless thread
This throbbing heart of joy and dread
With tremblings of the wayside grass
And pillars of the mountain pass
And circling of the stars extreme
In boundless heights of heaven.

I dream
My dark heart into earth, I heap
My spirit over with cold sleep,
Resign my senses, one by one,
To glooms that never saw the sun.
Fade from this self to what behind
Earth's myriad shapes is urging blind,
Am emptied of man's name, become
A blankness, as the mountain dumb.
If so I may attain to win
The secret thou art rooted in.

Can life renounce not life? Must still
The inexorably moving will
Seek and make rankle the dulled sting
Of essence? Must the desert spring
Revive, and the forgotten seed
Be drawn again by its old need
Through blind beginnings of a sense,

And dark desire of difference,
And fear, and hope that feeds on fear,
To its own destined character?
I cannot lose nor abdicate
The separateness of my state,
Nor thou, that out of burial drawn
Through the black earth didst shoot and dawn
Tender and small and green, and mount
In air, a springing, silent fount,
Until the cold bud, sheathed so long,
Slow swelled and burst like sudden song
Into the sun's delight, and naught
Of costliest tissue ever wrought.
Fragrant and in rare colours dyed.
For the white body of a bride
Or king's anointing feast, could so
Enrich the noon or inly glow
To lose the sweetly-kindled sense
In mystery of magnificence.

Was there no cost to make thee fair?
Did no far-off long pains prepare
Those clustered curves of incense-breath?
Did nothing suffer unto death
To poise thee in thy glory? Came
No tinge upon thy coloured flame
From sighs? Was there no bosom bled
That thou mightest be perfected —
As, serving his taskmaster's doom
A brown slave patient at the loom
Toils, weaving some fine web of gold,
More precious than his race, to fold
In soft attire an idle queen,
When long his own thin hands have been
Dust, but in all their toil arrayed
She through her pillared palace-shade
Glows flower-like, and her young gaze has
No thought of any deep Alas!
Threaded into the sumptuous vest
That lies upon her perfumed breast;
Or as at crimsoned eve on high
Some dying warrior turns his eye
Where, lifted over spear and sword
Among the loud victorious horde,
A golden trophy gleams with blood
That from his own spent body flowed,
And trumpets sound across the sand
To sunset in a conquered land?

O thou wast from life's weltering ore
Breathed by enchanting mind before
Man was in his own shape. Far, far
Thou seemest as the evening star!
Yet movest me like that lone light
Fetched through the ages of the night
Into this breathing garden-close;
Or like the things that no man knows
In a child's eyes; or like, for one
Watching a seaward-sinking sun,
Beyond cold wastes of water pale
The dim communion of a sail.
Ah! though I know not what thou art,
Yet in the fastness of my heart
How shall I tell what lies unwrought
Into the figured films of thought,
Uncoloured yet by sharp or sweet,
Or what forge of transforming heat
Threatens this world of use and fact
Wherewith the busy brain is packed?
Thou art of me, O Flower of Flame,
What is not uttered, has no name.
The springing of a want unmated,
A joy no fallen hour has dated.
Some of my mystery thou boldest.
Secretly, splendidly unfoldest.

THE BOWL OF WATER

She is eight years old.
When she laughs, her eyes laugh;
Light dances in her eyes;
She tosses back her long hair
And with a song replies;
Then on light feet she darts away
Tripping, mischievously gay.
But now into this room of shadow
Coming slowly with the sun's long ray
And all the morning on her simple hair,
O how serious-eyed
She steps pre-occupied
Holding a bowl of water
Poised in her fingers' care, —
Water quivering with cool gleams
And wavering and a-roll

Within the clear glass bowl,
That brimmed and luminous seems
A wonder and a shining secrecy,
As if it were the world's most precious thing.
So open-clear that all have passed it by.
Cut stalks of iris lie
On the bare table, flowers and swelling buds
Clasped in close curves up to the purple tips
That shall to-morrow burst
And shoot a splendid wing,
When they have drawn into their veins the spring
Which those young hands, with the drops bright on them.
So all intently bring;
Costless felicity,
Living and unbought!
But over me, O flowers
That neither ask nor sigh,
Comes the thought.
How all this world is wanting and athirst!

FERRY HINKSEY

Beyond the ferry water
That fast and silent flowed,
She turned, she gazed a moment,
Then took her onward road

Between the winding willows
To a city white with spires
It seemed a path of pilgrims
To the home of earth's desires.

Blue shade of golden branches
Spread for her journeying.
Till he that lingered lost her
Among the leaves of Spring.

IN THE FOREST

The beeches towering high
Greenly cloud the sky.
The shadows all are green
With living sun unseen.
O wonderful the sound

Of green leaves all around,
When nothing yet is heard
Of windy branches stirred
But wavering lights alone
Innumerably blown
Come trembling, and then cease
Upon a trembling peace.
What breathed in it? A sigh?
Or something yet more shy
Of speech? A spirit-kiss?
A waft of fairy bliss
That seeks for voice on our
Lips, there to find its flower
In some sweet syllable?
O Love, I cannot tell;
But light brims in your eyes
And makes divine replies.

THE FOREST PINE

A hundred autumns fallen in fire
To dust and mould
Have faded from their perished gold
To throne thee higher,
O Titan pine, that soarest straight
From ground to sky without a mate.
Like one desire.

Dark is the hollow as a cup
Of shadow immense,
Of daylight-daunting dimness, whence
Thou springest up
Far into light, to take thy fill
Of splendour, solitary in still
Magnificence.

Leaves of the low brake hide a stir
Of small soft things:
Life, busy in flit of secret wings
And slinking fur,
Pricks buried seeds that upward thrust.
And green through germinating dust
Triumphant stings.

But thou, that seemest earth to scorn
And air to claim.

With all thy plumy spire aflame
And crest upborne
In the blue air, so far, so high,
As if the silence of the sky
About thee came.

Thou hidest all the sappy stream
That in thee swells;
Motionless fibre nothing tells:
And thou dost seem
To tower in glorious ignorance
Of earth's small stir and chafe, a trance,
A soaring dream!

And in a trance thou boldest me
With bated will;
And I am still, as thou art still,
My spirit free.
My body charm-dissolved to naught
But the vibration of a thought,
If thought could be.

O hush! within the blood is felt
An airy fear,
A faltering; and the heart can hear
The silence melt
To something frailer than a sound
Borne from the wide horizon's bound
To the inward ear.

Slowly, ah! slowly, a hush begins,
A trembling, where
Those branches sleep on golden air,
And gradual wins
A voice, a music, a long surge.
Sweet as a song, sad as a dirge.
Sighed out like prayer!

The singer knows not what he sings.
A lonely sound
Comes trembling through him from profound
Aerial springs.
The songs, the sighs, the world exiled,
Seek him and in his heart-throbs wild
Still their wild wings.

FIDE ET LITERIS

(Written for the fourth centenary of St Paul's School)

When the long-clouded spirit of Europe drew
Life from Greek springs, frost could no longer bind,
And old truth shone like fresh dawn on the blind,
Our Founder sowed his pregnant seed: he knew
No crabbed rule; rather he chose a clue
That should emband us of our historied kind
Comrades, and keep in us a morning mind.
Since to the wise Learning is always New.
In Faith and Letters he enshrined his light;
Faith, the divine adventure that holds on
Through this world's forest into worlds unknown,
And Letters, that since speech on earth began
As one unended sentence burning write
The hope, the triumph, and the tears of Man.

PAST AND FUTURE

Past is the past! But no, it is not past,
In us, in us, it quickens, wants, aspires;
And on our hearts the unknown dead have cast
The hunger and the thirst of their desires.

Unknown the pangs, bhe peace we too prepare!
What shakes this bosom shall reverberate
Through ages unconceived: in that deep lair
The unguessed, unhoped, undreaded issues wait.

Our pregnant acts are all unprophesied.
We dream sublime conclusions; destine, plan.
Build and unbuild; yet turn no jot aside
The something infinite that moves in Man.

We write The End where fate has scarce begun;
And no man knows the thing that he has done.

THUNDER ON THE DOWNS

Wide earth, wide heaven, and in the summer air
Silence! The summit of the Down is bare
Between the climbing crests of wood; but those

Great sea-winds, wont, when the wet South-West blows,
To rock tall beeches and strong oaks aloud
And strew torn leaves upon the streaming cloud,
To-day are idle, slumbering far aloof.
Under the solemn height and gorgeous roof
Of cloud-built sky, all earth is indolent.
Wandering hum of bees and thymy scent
Of the short turf enrich pure loneliness;
Scarcely an airy topmost-twining tress
Of bryony quivers where the thorn it wreathes;
Hot fragrance from the honeysuckle breathes.
And sweet the rose floats on the arching briar's
Green fountain, sprayed with delicate frail fires.
For clumps of thicket, dark beneath the blaze
Of the high westering sun, beset the ways
Of smooth grass narrowing where the slope runs steep
Down to green woods, and glowing shadows keep
A freshness round the mossy roots, and cool
The light that sleeps as in a chequered pool
Of golden air. O woods, I love you well,
I love the flowers you hide, your ferny smell;
But here is sweeter solitude, for here
My heart breathes heavenly space; the sky is near
To thought, with heights that fathomlessly glow;
And the eye wanders the wide land below.

And this is England! June's undarkened green
Gleams on far woods; and in the vales between
Grey hamlets, older than the trees that shade
Their ripening meadows, are in quiet laid,
Themselves a part of the warm, fruitful ground.
The little hills of England rise around;
The little streams that wander from them shine
And with their names remembered names entwine
Of old renown and honour, fields of blood
High causes fought on, stubborn hardihood
For freedom spent, and songs, our noblest pride,
That in the heart of England never died.
And burning still make splendour of our tongue.
Glories enacted, spoken, suffered, sung,
You lie emblazoned on this land now sleeping;
And southward, over leagues of forest sweeping
White on the verge glistens the famous sea.
That English wave, on which so haughtily
Towered her sails, and one sail homeward bore
Past capes of silently lamenting shore
Victory's dearest dead. O shores of home,
Since by the vanished watch-fire shields of Rome

Dinted this upland turf, what hearts have ached
To see you far away, what eyes have waked
Ere dawn to watch those cliffs of long desire
One after one rise in their voiceless choir
Out of the twilight over the rough blue
Like music! . . .

But now heavy gleams imbrue
The inland air: breathless the valleys hold
Their colours in a veil of sultry gold
With mingled shadows that have ceased to crawl;
For far in heaven is thunder! Over all
A single cloud in slow magnificence
Climbs like a mountain, gradual and immense,
With awful head unstirring, and moved on
Against the zenith, towers above the sun.
And still it thickens luminous fold on fold
Of fatal colour, ominously scrolled
And fleeced with fire; above the sun it towers
Like some vast thought quickening a world not ours
Remote in the waste blue, as if behind
Its rim were splendour that could smite us blind,
So doom-piled and intense it crests heaven's height
And mounting makes a menace of the light.

A menace! Yes, for when light comes, we fear.
Light that may touch, as the pure angel-spear.
Us to ourselves, make visible, make start
The apparition of the very heart
And mystery of our thoughts, awaked from under
The mask of cheating habit, and to thunder
Bare in a moment of white fire what we
Have feared and fled, our own reality.

And if a lightning now were loosed in flame
Out of the darkness of the cloud to claim
Thy heart, O England, how wouldst thou be known
In that hour? How to the quick core be shown
And seen? What cry shoiild from thy very soul
Answer the judgment of that thunder-roll!

I hear a voice arraign thee. "Where is now
The exaltation that once lit thy brow?
Thou countest all thy ocean-sundered lands,
Thou heapest up the labours of thy hands,
Thou seest all thy ships upon the seas.
But in thine own heart mean idolatries
Usurp devotion, choke thee and annul

Noble excess of spirit, and make dull
Thine eyes, enfleshed with much dominion.
Art thou so great and is the glory gone?
Do these bespeak thy freedom who deflower
Time, and make barren every senseless hour.
Who from themselves hurry, like men afraid
Lest what they are be to themselves betrayed?
Or those who in their huddled thousands sweat
To buy the sleep that helps them to forget? —
Life lies unused, life with its loveliness!
While the cry ravens still, ' Possess, Possess! '
And there is no possession. All the lust
Of gainful man is quieted in dust;
His faith, his fear, his joy, his doom he owns.
No more: the rest is parcelled with his bones
Save what the imagination of his heart
Can to the labour of his hands impart.
Making stones serve his spirit's desire, and breathe.
But thou, what dost thou to the world bequeath.
Who gatherest riches in a waste of mind
Unto what end, confidently blind.
Forgetful of the things that grow not old
And alone live and are not bought or sold?"

Speaks that voice truth? Is it for this that great
And tender spirits suffered scorn and hate.
Loved to the utmost, poured themselves, gave all
Nor counted cost, spirits imperial?
Where are they now, they that our memory guard
Among the nations? Shall I say enstarred
And throned aloof? No, not from heavens of thought
Watching our muddied brief procession, not
Judges sublime above us, without share
In our thronged ways of struggle, hope, despair.
But in our blood, our dreams, our deeds they stir.
Strive on our lips for language, shame and spur
The sluggard in us, out of darkness come
Like summoned champions when the world is dumb;
Within our hearts they wait with all they gave:
Woe to us, woe, if we become their grave!
It shall not be. Darken thy pall, and trail.
Thunder of heaven, above the valleys pale!
Another England in my vision glows.
And she is armed within; at last she knows
Herself, and what to her own soul belongs.
Mid the world's irremediable wrongs
She keeps her faith; and nothing of her name
Or of her handiwork but doth proclaim

Her purpose. Her own soul hath made her free,
Not circumstance; she knows no victory
Save of the mind: in her is nothing done,
No wrong, no shame, no glory of any one.
But is the cause of all and each, a thing
Felt like a fire to kindle and to sting
The proud blood of a nation. On her brows
Is hope; her body doth her spirit house
Express and eloquent, not dumb and frore;
And her voice echoes over sea and shore.
And all the lands and isles that are her own
In choric interchange and antiphon
Answer, as fancy hears in yonder cloud
From vale to vale repeated low and loud
The still-suspended thunder.

Hearts of Youth,
High-beating, ardent, quick in hope and ruth
And noble anger, O wherever now
You dedicate your uncorrupted vow
To be an energy of Light, a sword
Of the ever-living Will, amid abhorred
Din of the reeking street and populous den
Where under the great stars blind lusts of men
War on each other, or escaped to hills
Where peace the solitary evening fills,
Or far remote on other soils of earth
Keeping the dearness of your fathers' hearth
On vast plains of the West, or Austral strands
Of the warm under-world, or storied lands
Of the orient sun, or over ocean ways
Stemming the wave through blue or stormy days.
Wherever, as the circling light slopes round,
On human lips is heard an English sound,
O scattered, silent, hidden and unknown.
Be lifted up, for you are not alone!
High-beating hearts, to your deep vows be true!
Live out your dreams, for England lives in you.

THE TRAM

(In the Midlands)

I

A grinding swerve, a hissing spurt,

And then a droning through the dirt!
The tram glides on its wonted way
Of everyday, of everyday.
Past every corner still the same
Squat houses huddle, meanly serried,
An image of the mute and maim
With life behind their windows buried;
Blank windows staring under slate
That presses on them desolate
As eyes bereft of brows, and drips
On puddled, flowerless garden strips.

Is it evening, noon or morn?
Is it Autumn, is it Spring?
Nothing tells but the forlorn
Rain that is over everything.
A rain that seems too slow to fall
And drifts, an immaterial pall
Of wetness in the air; it leaves
A dismal glistening on the eaves,
And grimed upon the pavement lies.
For the dirt is in the very skies.

Like without, and like within!
Dull bodies clatter out and in.
And the beU clangs, as they subside
On the long seat, and on we glide,
Defensive creatures, all askance
At one another! Small eyes lance
Suspicion; fingers tighten close
On baskets; thin lips will not lose
A word too much, and skirts draw shy
From any touch too neighbourly.
And now a bald-head, grossly quaking
And lurching round for elbow space.
Sets a black-beaded bonnet shaking
Above a pinched averted face
Or stiffly-bastioned heaving bust
That virtuously expands distrust.

And all the fluttered narrow looks
Appear like little painful books
Of soiled accounts, where bargains keep
Their cherished tale of capture cheap.
For life is all a cheapening,
And the rain is over everything,
And there is neither mirth nor woe.
Who made it so, who made it so?

II

As I muse, as I muse,
Numbed at heart, with eyelids leaden,
Stupefying senses lose
All but sounds and sights that deaden;
Glassy gaze and shuffled feet,
Humid glide of the endless street,
Passing by with rank on rank
Of dripping roofs and windows blank,
Till one dull motion drones the brain
Out of meaning, out of time.
And the blood beats to a chime
As of bells with mouth inane.

And now a monstrous ark it seems
That's hurried with the speed of dreams
Through streets of ages! On it drives
Among unnumbered years and lives.
And now the sound grows like a surging,
As if this speed a host were urging,
And in the sound are voices coming
Thick, and tumultuous music drumming;
And savage odours are astir
Of forest leaves and hidden fur,
And naked limbs of hunters glide
And warriors in the great sun ride,
And mutinous-nostrilled horses champing
With restless necks are strongly stamping.
The Roman purple passes proud
Like an eagle through a cloud.
Lo, knights-at-arms with pennons dancing
To death's adventure gay advancing,
And here a queen that is a bride
Crimson-robed and lonely-eyed,
And there a pilgrim's dusty feet
Faring to the heavenly city;
And now an idle beggar singing
How the sun and wind are sweet,
A wayside song, a wanderer's ditty:
And still around, out of the ground.
The armies of the dead are springing;
And with unearthly speed and number
Compelled like those that walk in slumber
They follow, follow! And at my ear
An imp that squats with demon leer

Is screaming, See the Triumph go!
See for whom the trumpets blow!
The prophesied, that goes before us!
This is he, Time's crown and wonder
That has the very stars for plunder;
This is he, the Promethean,
(Hark the ever-rolling paean
With a wilderness of apes for chorus!)
Who fetched from heaven the stormy fire
To serve and toil for his desire.
And plumbed the globe, and spoiled old Earth
Of all the secrets of her birth;
See him, throned triumphant there,
Like a toad, with glassy stare;
Eyes, and sees not; ears, and hears not!
Heart, and hopes not; soul, and fears not!

III

A boy with a bunch of primroses!
He sits uneasy, flushed of cheek.
With wandering eyes and does not speak.
His hands are hot; the flowers are his.

But Spring, O Spring is in the world.
And eager fancy forward flying
Sees little fronds almost uncurled
Where still the dead brown bracken 's lying,
And a thousand thousand shining drops
Upon the young leaves of the copse.
The spurge has all his green cups filled —
A gust will shake and brim them over —
From cuckoo-flowers the rain is spilled;
I smell first sweetness of the clover.
Long tendrils of the vetch are thirsting,
White blossom on the thorn is bursting;
Twigs redden on the sapling oaks
Above the grass that shoots and soaks;
The streams flow fast by reed and rush;
Loose notes come fluted from the thrush;
In forky boughs and leafy shade
There's busyness for every wing;
And sweet through stalk and root and blade
Run juices of the wine of Spring.
But the primrose perfume, faint and rare
Is like a sigh of Spring forsaken.
O shy soft beauty, torn and taken!

O delicate bruised tissue fair!
You are like the eyes of an outcast fond,
Or a face seen at a prison-grate:
For Beauty 's but a vagabond
And knows no home and has no mate.

IV

Alas! what dungeon walls we rear,
For our possession, round us here!
We make a castle of defence
Out of the dullness of the sense;
Possess our burrow like the mole;
And with the blundering hands of chance
Grow cruel in our ignorance.
What is another's springing soul
That I should seek to force and bind it?
To catch my gain where it has tripped,
To thrust it down when it has slipped,
To stupefy and dumb and blind it.
Fortress my virtue with its failing,
And kindle courage at its quailing?
What is another's thought, that I
Should wish it mine in effigy?
Ah! we that grasp and bind and tame
It is ourselves, ourselves we maim;
We maim the world. The very Spring
Stops all mute and will not sing,
The sapless branches will not quicken,
The cells of secret honey sicken.
Giant brambles writhe and twist
About the trees in poisonous mist.
The spider fattens; flies oppress.
And the buds are blackened promises,
Nothing stirs, but the leaf is shed,
And all the world of wonder 's dead!
O for the touch that shall awake!
O for the word that shall renew!
And all this crust of sense shall break
And the world of wonder pierce us through;
The scales be fallen from a sight
Ravished with fountains of delight.
And the sad dullness of our scorn
Be like remembered night at morn:
Then we shall feel what we have made
Of one another, and be afraid.

TOWERS OF ITALY

Never were towers so fair, so bold,
Passionately springing, arrogant towers!
Nor air so blue over roofs so old.
Nor on ancient walls so rare a gold,
When I found my love among the flowers.

O mighty Spirits, never to be stilled,
Whose glorious works concluded seem,
Yet in whom is a glory unfulfilled.
And still for us you build, you build.
What have you told her out of your dream?

She comes from shadow of streets below.
And surely, O Spirits, you were there.
Pacing among the shadows; lo.
In her eyes is a light, on her face a glow
As she comes through a golden air.

Do you feel, do you breathe and throb again
In her bosom's beat and shining eyes, —
As an old chant heavy with world-old pain
Is lifted afresh in a splendid strain
On young lips, up to the skies?

My love is fair as a voice that sings.
In a scented garden of joyous flowers.
Do the old walls keep their buried things?
Yet the air is astir as with throbbing of wings
And heaven with the springing of the towers.

The hills lift a loneliness around;
But my love has a light about her head;
And as if they uttered names renowned.
Bells from the towers to the silences resound —
Voices of the youth of the dead!

VIGIL

In the hallow of pale night upon the moor
The silence blows a perfume: O but hark!
A sound is in the bosom of the dark,
Breathed like a secret from the glimmering shore;

A vigil of unearthly sound, the sea
That never slumbers and begins anew.
And melts into our hearts amid the dew,
Murmuring on the moor to you and me.

Out of silence dateless is the old earth,
Before our heard or ever voice could frame
Speech, or the human dearness of a name.
To glorify man's longing or his mirth,
Ere ever any place was historied
For hearts that sever yet their own home keep,
That sound comes immemorial like sleep
Fresh, with the morning in dark softness hid.

O Love, O Love, were we not there, we too,
In far nights and wild silences? Were we
Not part of this old secret of the sea?
For O your kiss, thrilling my body through.
Touches me from eternity, as if I
And you were of the things before Time came
To measure men's desire and loss and shame.
And no use disenchants this mystery.

THE PORCH OF STARS

As in a porch of stars we stand; the night
Throbs through us, O Love, with its worlds of light,
And mingles us in glory of one breath,
One infinite ignorance of Time and Death.
Behold, I am dyed in thee, and thou in me;
We are the colours of infinity,
We are two flames that are one flame.
We are but Love, and have no name.
But did we part, O Love, if we could part,
The very blood were taken from my heart.
Time and Death would ride the night
Then, and ended were all light,
The stream of stars would fall like stone
And heaven's utmost height be darkened,
And we be lost, like dust that 's blown.
Like a cry, where none has hearkened.

THE PROMISE

What wonder of what hope dost thou enfold,
Whose eyes are all filled with futurity?
What shape of more than beauty dost thou mould
With desire's strength out of the dim to-be?

Thy bosom is the haunt of holy fears.
Shadows are all about thee, whispering
Deep words and glorious names from the full years;
But like the stars in heaven thy pulses sing

Of a voice sweeter than all tones yet heard;
Of a heart richer than the summer's store;
Of earth awakened from old bonds and spurred
To run a new race for her conqueror.

Thou waitest, thy thoughts glowing, like the Night;
And in thee buds the flower, the marvel. Light.

A MOTHER'S SONG

Over fast-closed baby eyes
In the garden's golden air
Blossom-white the butterflies
Hover, hurry, part and pair,
Sudden shinings, flown nowhere!
Blue, above, the unbounded skies!

Little one, downy head,
O fingers clasping, shaped and small.
Laid in soft nest of thy bed.
How the trees are Titan-tall
Over thee that sleepest, all
Ignorant of thy hope and dread!

O so small, and all around
Life so vast works wonders new.
Yet to thee is set no bound
What thou shalt desire and do,
Find and fashion and hold true;
Deeps thou hast no thought can sound:

Thou art sought by powers unknown;
On thy trembling heart-strings play
Airs unheard, O little one!
Whisperings of far away.
Music made of day and day —

Lands of promise, all thine own!

Wide as heaven the secrecies
Thou dost fold: ev'n now, ev'n here,
Thou dost touch infinities.
While o'er thee in hope, in fear,
My white wishes, far and near.
Hover like the butterflies.

ONE YEAR OLD

Is it we that are wise, is it we,
Who have bought with a price of grief
A wisdom seldom free
From scorn or disbelief.
Who find this world fulfil
An end that is not our will,
Who toil with the light in our eyes
Showing us scarce begun
The things we meant to have done,
Is it we, is it we, that are wise?

Or O, is it you, is it you,
That have yet no language of ours,
But whose eyes are a laiighter blue
As of light slipping under the showers,
Whose carol, sweeter than words.
Trills clear as an April bird's,
Or a dancing brook on the hill, —
Blithe springs of a confidence
That bubbles, we know not whence.
And has no knowledge of ill?

Lo, our desires have gone
Like ships to a future far
And vanished in mist alone
By no befriending star.
But all to you is a wonder
Fresh as the sky, whereunder
Life moves to pledge delight;
You need no hope to bear
The day through the day's care;
Your joys are all in sight.

You want not a word to tell
What lies beyond our guess

And springs like a sparkling well
In a lovely speechlessness.
And we that have shaped with art
Language of mind and of mart,
We have never yet found speech
For the heart's blood deepest stirred:
Something is flown with a word
Or is buried beneath our reach.

Our speech is spun from the pain
Of thought and heavy with years,
And dyed with an ancient stain
From passion and blood and tears.
But O, I vow, when I hear
Your wordless carol clear,
I would cast this speech that endures
As a sorry old patchwork coat,
Could I but re-fill my throat
With the liquid joy in yours.

BECAUSE THOU ART NEAREST

Because thou art nearest
To the mystery of the fire
That is Earth's and the soul's
And the body's desire,
Whereof we were made
As a song out of sound,
Trembling together
And together enwound,
O frailer, more fading
The hope and the lure
That are not where thou art: —
They fade nor endure.
But in thee is the secret,
The star, and the fire.
Ever nearer and dearer,
My joy, my desire.

SEVEN YEARS

Seven years have flown like seven days,
Like seven days of shining weather,
Since we, forsaking single ways,

Trod earth and faced the skies together.
The old is new, the new is old,
And who shall reckon, one or seven.
The years that Time has never told?
He numbers not the days of Heaven.

SORROW

Woe to him that has not known the woe of man,
Who has not felt within him burning all the want
Of desolated bosoms, since the world began;
Felt, as his own, the burden of the fears that daunt;
Who has not eaten failure's bitter bread, and been
Among those ghosts of hope that haunt the day, unseen.

Only when we are hurt with all the hurt untold, —
In us the thirst, the hunger, and ours the helpless hands.
The palsied effort vain, the darkness and the cold, —
Then, only then, the Spirit knows and understands,
And finds in every sigh breathed out beneath the sun
The human heart that makes us infinitely one.

E. H. P: IN MEMORY

Home from the wounds of Earth and wasting Time
The marvel of her beauty and morning prime
She has taken glorious with the dew of youth
Still on her thoughts, those thoughts that from her eyes
Gleamed still or splendid, unafraid of truth;
All her white passion, all the secrecies
Of wild, sweet fire that her heart guarded, all
Her heart's young rose, ere yet one leaf could fade or fall!

She that was made like a song nobly wrought
In fine, fair mould of movement, speech and thought,
With glory of hair about the buoyant head; —
In breaking voices we her beauty tell:
But she is radiant, she is perfected.
Where our long hopes far from our sorrows dwell,
A song unended, but a song so sweet,
No tongue of mortal dares its melody complete.

Laurence Binyon – A Short Biography

Robert Laurence Binyon, CH, was born on August 10th, 1869 in Lancaster in Lancashire, England to Quaker parents, Frederick Binyon and Mary Dockray.

He studied at St Paul's School, London before enrolling at Trinity College, Oxford, to read classics.

Binyon's first published work was Persephone in 1890. Whilst only a few pages in length it certainly illustrated the talents that Binyon would develop as a poet even though he continued to advance multiple career opportunities.

Immediately after graduating in 1893, Binyon started work at the British Museum for the Department of Printed Books, writing catalogues for the museum and art monographs for himself. As well as being one of England's best poets he was also renowned for his knowledge of various arts particularly with regard to Japan and Persia.

His first poetry book Lyric Poems was published in 1894.

In 1895 his first art book, Dutch Etchers of the Seventeenth Century, was published and, that same year, Binyon moved into the Museum's Department of Prints and Drawings.

Whilst Binyon became known to a wide audience as a poet his output was not prodigious. In 1898, Porphyrion & Other Poems was published followed by Odes (1901) and The Death of Adam & Other Poems (1904).

That same year, 1904, Binyon married the historian Cicely Margaret Powell. The union was to produce three daughters.

In the early years of the 20th Century Binyon was a regular patron of the Wiener Cafe of London together with fellow artists and intellectuals; Ezra Pound, Sir William Rothenstein, Walter Sickert, Charles Ricketts, Lucien Pissarro and Edmund Dulac.

His poetic work continued despite the demands of the British Museum and his other interests. London Visions was published in 1908 followed by England & Other Poems in 1909.

His work at the British Museum ensured promotions were a frequent occurrence for Binyon. In 1909, he became its Assistant Keeper, and in 1913 he was made the Keeper of the new Sub-Department of Oriental Prints and Drawings.

It was also at this time that he played a crucial role in the formation of Modernism in London by introducing young Imagist poets such as Ezra Pound, Richard Aldington and H.D. (Hilda Doolittle) to East Asian visual art and literature.

Many of Binyon's books produced while at the Museum were influenced by his own sensibilities as a poet, although some are clearly works of plain scholarship, such as his four volume catalogue of all the Museum's English drawings, and his seminal catalogue of Chinese and Japanese prints.

Binyon's poetic reputation before the war, although built on several slim volumes, was such that, on the death of the Poet Laureate Alfred Austin in 1913, Binyon was among the names considered as his likely successor. It was quite a field. Among the other illustrious contenders were Thomas Hardy, John Masefield and Rudyard Kipling; however the post was awarded to Robert Bridges.

Moved and shaken by the onset of the World War I and its military tactics of young men slaughtered to hold or gain a few yards of shell-shocked mud as the British Expeditionary Force began its campaign Binyon wrote his seminal poem For the Fallen, with its Ode of Remembrance (the third and fourth or simply the fourth stanza of the poem). The poem was published by The Times newspaper on September 21st, when public feeling was shaken by the recent Battle of Marne. It became an instant classic, turning moments of great loss into a National and human tribute.

Today, For the Fallen, is often recited at Remembrance Sunday services as well as being an integral part of Anzac Day services in Australia and New Zealand and of November 11th Remembrance Day services in Canada. The "Ode of Remembrance" is now acknowledged as a tribute to all casualties of war, irrespective of nation.

In 1915, despite being too old to enlist, Binyon volunteered at a British hospital for French soldiers, the Hôpital Temporaire d'Arc-en-Barrois, Haute-Marne, France, working for a short time as a hospital orderly.

He returned there in the summer of 1916 and took care of soldiers taken in from the Verdun battlefield. He wrote about his experiences in For Dauntless France (1918) and his poems, "Fetching the Wounded" and "The Distant Guns", were inspired by his hospital service.

After the war, he returned to the British Museum and wrote numerous books on art; especially on William Blake, Persian and Japanese art. His work on ancient Japanese and Chinese cultures offered inspiration that inspired many, among them the poets Ezra Pound and W. B. Yeats. His work on Blake and his followers kept alive the then nearly-forgotten memory of the work of Samuel Palmer. Binyon's spectrum of interests continued the traditional interest of British visionary Romanticism in the rich strangeness of Mediterranean and Oriental cultures.

In 1931, his two volume Collected Poems appeared and by 1932, Binyon was promoted to the post of Keeper of the Prints and Drawings Department. The following year, 1933, he retired from the British Museum. He went to live in the country at Westridge Green, near Streatley but continued writing poetry.

In 1933–1934, Binyon was appointed Norton Professor of Poetry at Harvard University. He delivered a series of lectures on The Spirit of Man in Asian Art, which were published in 1935.

Binyon continued his academic work: in May, 1939 he gave the prestigious Romanes Lecture in Oxford on Art and Freedom, and in 1940 he was appointed the Byron Professor of English Literature at the University of Athens. He worked there until forced to leave by the German invasion of Greece in April, 1941.

Binyon had been friends with Ezra Pound for a long time, and in the 1930s the two became especially close; Pound affectionately called him "BinBin", and he assisted Binyon with his translation of Dante.

Between 1933 and 1943, Binyon published his acclaimed translation of Dante's Divine Comedy in an English version of terza rima, made with some editorial assistance by Ezra Pound. It was acknowledged for many decades as *the* popular translation for Dante readers.

During the horrors of the Second World War Binyon wrote a poem that many claim as to be a masterpiece 'The Burning of the Leaves', puts in print his lines on the London Blitz.

At his death Binyon was working on a major three-part Arthurian trilogy, the first part of which was published after his death as The Madness of Merlin (1947).

Robert Laurence Binyon died in Dunedin Nursing Home, Bath Road, Reading, on March 10th, 1943 after undergoing an operation. A funeral service was held at Trinity College Chapel, Oxford, on March 13th, 1943.

Binyon's ashes were scattered at St. Mary's Church, Aldworth.

On November 11th, 1985, Binyon was among sixteen poets of the Great War commemorated on a slate stone unveiled in Westminster Abbey's Poets' Corner. The inscription on the stone quotes a fellow Great War poet, Wilfred Owen. It reads: "My subject is War, and the pity of War. The Poetry is in the pity."

Laurence Binyon – A Concise Bibliography

Poems and Verse
Persephone (1890)
Lyric Poems (1894)
The Praise of Life (1896)
Porphyrion & Other Poems (1898)
Odes (1901)
Death of Adam & Other Poems (1904)
Penthesilea (1905)
London Visions (1908)
England & Other Poems (1909)
Auguries (1913)
For The Fallen (The Times, September 21st, 1914)
The Winnowing Fan (1914)
The Anvil (1916)
The Cause (1917)
The New World: Poems (1918)
The Secret: Sixty Poems (1920)
The Idols (1928)
Collected Poems Vol I: London Visions, Narrative Poems, Translations (1931)
Collected Poems Vol II: Lyrical Poems (1931)
The North Star & Other Poems (1941)
The Burning of the Leaves & Other Poems (1944)
The Madness of Merlin (1947)

Poems Set to Music

In 1915 Cyril Rootham set "For the Fallen" for chorus and orchestra, first performed in 1919 by the Cambridge University Musical Society conducted by the composer.

Edward Elgar set to music "The Fourth of August", "To Women", and "For the Fallen", as The Spirit of England, Op. 80, for tenor or soprano solo, chorus and orchestra (1917).

English Arts and Myth

Dutch Etchers of the Seventeenth Century (1895), Binyon's first book on painting
John Crone and John Sell Cotman (1897)
William Blake: Being all his Woodcuts Photographically Reproduced in Facsimile (1902)
English Poetry in its relation to painting and the other arts (1918)
Drawings and Engravings of William Blake (1922)
Arthur: A Tragedy (1923)
The Followers of William Blake (1925)
The Engraved Designs of William Blake (1926)
Landscape in English Art and Poetry (1931)
English Watercolours (1933)
Gerard Hopkins and his influence (1939)
Art and freedom. (The Romanes lecture, delivered 25 May 1939). Oxford: The Clarendon press, (1939)

Japanese and Persian Arts

Painting in the Far East (1908)
Japanese Art (1909)
Flight of the Dragon (1911)
The Court Painters of the Grand Moguls (1921)
Japanese Colour Prints (1923)
The Poems of Nizami (1928) (Translation)
Persian Miniature Painting (1933)
The Spirit of Man in Asian Art (1936)
Autobiography[edit]
For Dauntless France (1918) (War memoir)

Biography

Botticelli (1913)
Akbar (1932)

Stage Plays

Brief Candles A verse-drama about the decision of Richard III to dispatch his two nephews
Paris and Œnone. A Tragedy in One Act (1906)
Godstow Nunnery: Play
Boadicea; A Play in eight Scenes
Attila: A Tragedy in Four Acts (1907)

Ayuli: A Play in three Acts and an Epilogue
Sophro the Wise: A Play for Children
(Most of the above were written for John Masefield's theatre).

www.ingramcontent.com/pod-product-compliance
Lightning Source LLC
Chambersburg PA
CBHW070112070426
42448CB00038B/2577